ICE HOCKEY LEGENDS

Martin Brodeur

Sergei Fedorov

Peter Forsberg

Wayne Gretzky

Dominik Hasek

Brett Hull

Jaromir Jagr

Paul Kariya

John LeClair

Mario Lemieux

Eric Lindros

Mark Messier

CHELSEA HOUSE PUBLISHERS

ICE HOCKEY LEGENDS

DOMINIK HASEK

Michael Burgan

CHELSEA HOUSE PUBLISHERS
Philadelphia

CB
Hasek

CR

Produced by P. M. Gordon Associates
Philadelphia, Pennsylvania

Picture research by Gillian Speeth, Picture This

CHELSEA HOUSE PUBLISHERS

Editor in Chief: Stephen Reginald
Managing Editor: James Gallagher
Production Manager: Pamela Loos
Art Director: Sara Davis
Director of Photography: Judy L. Hasday
Senior Production Editor: Lisa Chippendale
Publishing Coordinator: James McAvoy
Project Editor: Becky Durost Fish
Cover Design and Digital Illustration: Keith Trego

Cover Photos: AP/Wide World Photos

The Chelsea House World Wide Web site address is
http://www.chelseahouse.com

First Printing

1 3 5 7 9 8 6 4 2

Library of Congress Cataloging-in-Publication Data

Burgan, Michael.
   Dominik Hasek / Michael Burgan.
      p. cm. — (Ice hockey legends)
   Includes bibliographical references (p.) and index.
   Summary: A biography of goaltender Dominik Hasek, the
Buffalo Sabres' "Dominator" and the National Hockey
League's Most Valuable Player in 1997.
   ISBN 0-7910-5014-9 (hardcover)
   1. Hasek, Dominik, 1965– —Juvenile literature. 2. Hockey
players—Czech Republic—Biography—Juvenile literature.
3. Buffalo Sabres (Hockey team)—Juvenile literature.
[1. Hasek, Dominik, 1965– 2. Hockey players.] I. Title.
II. Series.
GV848.5.H38B87 1998
796.962'092—dc21   98-37678
[B]   CIP
                                                           AC

CONTENTS

Dominik Hasek stood in front of the goal wearing his pads, gloves, and mask, the tools of the trade for a hockey goalie. But instead of playing for his usual team, the Buffalo Sabres, Hasek was representing his homeland, the Czech Republic, at the 1998 winter Olympics in Nagano, Japan. With Hasek playing brilliantly in goal, the Czechs had reached the semifinals.

In the quarterfinal round, the Czechs had beaten the United States, 4–1, with Hasek stopping 38 shots. Entering the semifinals, he had allowed only five goals in four contests. Hasek and his teammates now faced Canada, the team favored to win the gold medal.

For the first time ever, National Hockey League (NHL) players had been allowed to enter the Olympics. The Canadian team was loaded with NHL stars, including Wayne Gretzky, Eric Lindros, Patrick Roy, and Ray Bourque. Only about half of

A taste of gold: Dominik Hasek enjoys his gold medal at the 1998 winter Olympics in Nagano, Japan.

the Czechs were from the NHL, but the Czech team had something no one else did: Hasek, "the Dominator," the man many consider the best goalie in the NHL.

Standing 5'11", Hasek (pronounced HA-shik) weighs just 168 pounds. One journalist, describing Hasek's thin neck and protruding ribs, compared him to the scarecrow in *The Wizard of Oz*. When former Buffalo teammate Garry Galley saw Hasek for the first time, he could not believe that the gangly guy in front of him was the great Dominik Hasek. But Galley soon learned that, in Hasek's case, looks truly were deceiving: "He may not look like much of an athlete, but he's a great goalie."

Hasek hoped to prove his talents once again in Nagano. The Czechs took a 1–0 lead, and Hasek managed to shut out the Canadians for almost the entire game. But with only about a minute to play, Trevor Linden finally got the puck past the Dominator. The teams played a scoreless 10-minute overtime, then began a shoot-out to determine a winner.

In a shoot-out, the five best scorers from each team go one-on-one against the opposing goalie. The team with the most goals wins. "You make one mistake, you lose the game," Hasek said later. "It's unbelievable pressure. The biggest pressure of my career."

That career had begun in Czechoslovakia (now two nations, the Czech Republic and Slovakia) before Hasek came to the United States in 1990. Since becoming the starting goalie for the Sabres in 1993, Hasek had won three Vezina Trophies, given each year to the best goalie in the NHL. In 1997 he had won both the Vezina and the league's Most Valuable Player (MVP) award—the first time

In the semifinal game at the Olympics, Hasek makes a save against Rod Brind'Amour of the favored Canadian team.

in 35 years that a goalie had earned the MVP honor—and he was on his way to repeating his sweep of those two awards in 1998.

Throughout his career, Hasek has been noted for his unusual goaltending style. One former coach said, "He flops around the ice like some fish." Most goalies try to stay on their feet, or at least remain vertical when they drop to their knees. Not Hasek. He sprawls and dives all over the crease, the goalie's designated area in front of the net. He is blessed with an incredibly flexible body, the result, he believes, of back exercises he did as a child. One teammate compared him to Gumby.

Goalies, moreover, are supposed to hold on to their sticks. But Hasek often drops his, then covers the puck with his blocker, the huge padded glove used to hold the stick. No matter how strange and unorthodox he might look on the ice, Hasek does what he's supposed to do: stop the puck.

Yet none of Hasek's NHL honors made a bit of difference in the Olympic shoot-out. It was a brand-new test for the Dominator—perhaps the defining moment of his career—as the best one-on-one scorers from Canada took turns loosing the puck at him.

Hasek first faced the speedy Theo Fleury. "I expected some fast move," Hasek said afterward. Fleury skated toward Hasek's right and flipped a high shot. Hasek followed his every move. The puck glanced off Hasek's shoulder and over the net. Save for Hasek.

At the other end of the ice, Hasek's teammate Robert Reichel beat Canadian goalie Patrick Roy, giving the Czechs a 1–0 advantage. Now the pressure was on for Hasek to hold the lead.

The next Canadian shooter was defenseman Ray Bourque. He ripped a hard shot to Hasek's left. With a flick of his glove, Hasek knocked the puck over the net. Joe Nieuwendyk was Hasek's next opponent. The Canadian came in close and tried to stuff in a backhand shot, but Hasek dropped to his knees butterfly-style (his legs spread out to either side) and stopped the shot. The score was still 1–0.

The hulking, hard-hitting Eric Lindros took the next shot for Canada. He raced in, faked to the right, then went to the left. Hasek fell to his back in front of the goal, his glove hand high in the air. Luckily for the Czechs, the shot went off the goalpost and wide of the net.

Canada's last chance fell to Brendan Shanahan. He tried to fake out Hasek, but then was too close to the net to get off a good shot. "My glove was there," Hasek later said. "My pad was there. What could he do?"

With that save, Hasek had preserved the win for the Czech Republic. Canadian coach Marc Crawford declared, "History will say this was a great game. It will go down as a classic."

And Hasek's play was the highlight of that classic. Shutting down five of hockey's best scorers during the shoot-out showed the world how truly great he is. But Hasek and his teammates still had one game to go, against the Russians, to win the gold medal.

In earlier years, when Russia was part of the Soviet Union, Russian players had helped make the Soviets the greatest Olympic hockey team ever. In 1998, though, the Russians lacked some of their best players. Still, they had already beaten the Czechs once in Nagano and might have been favored to win the gold—if Hasek had not been playing so well.

For two periods, the teams skated to a scoreless tie. Then, with 11:52 to go in the game, Petr Svoboda scored for the Czechs. Hasek played flawlessly. He didn't have to make many great saves, but his reputation alone was a factor. Russian coach Vladimir Yurvinov said, "He made a major psychological impact, because at times I felt we were not quite sure if we could score at all."

Hasek stopped all 20 Russian shots. The Czechs held on for a 1–0 win—and the gold medal. When the final horn sounded, Czech gloves, sticks, and

The Czech players, with Hasek in front, pose with their gold medals at the Nagano Olympics.

helmets went flying into the air, and the players swarmed Hasek at the net. In six games, he had stopped 148 of 154 shots for an amazing .961 save percentage.

Most hockey fans were ready to agree with Svoboda, who said, "He's unbelievable; he's the best goalie I've ever seen, and I don't think anyone else can come close to him." Hasek, however, was modest about his performance: "My job is to give up less goals than my team scores. Today we scored only one so I had to stop all of the pucks."

After the Olympics, Hasek attended a celebration in Prague, capital of the Czech Republic. With fireworks crisscrossing the sky, about 150,000 cheering fans welcomed home their hockey heroes. Some chanted "Hasek for President." The Dominator was not ready to give up hockey for politics, but he was glad that he had played so well for his homeland. "This was about playing for the Czech Republic," he said, "and for the people who taught me how to play hockey."

LIFE IN CZECHOSLOVAKIA

For the citizens of Pardubice (pronounced Par-doo-BIT-seh), Czechoslovakia, hockey was a way of life. An industrial city east of Prague, Pardubice in the 1970s and 1980s was the home of Tesla, one of the best professional teams in the country. The city's fans were devoted to Tesla, and young boys from miles around dreamed of playing for the team. To prepare for a shot at the pros, these budding hockey stars learned the game in the city's various junior leagues.

Dominik Hasek was born in Pardubice on January 29, 1965. For the first few years of his life, he and his family lived with his grandparents. Hasek's father, Jan, was a miner who worked 100 miles away; he lived with the family only on weekends. Hasek developed a close relationship with his grandfather, who helped the young goalie sharpen his skills by shooting tennis balls at him. Even then, Dominik knew what position he wanted to play. "Ever since I can remember," Hasek

---

Hasek in 1987 proudly wears the uniform of the Czech national team.

recalled years later, "I always made straight for the goal—in soccer, in hockey, in everything."

Hasek excelled in soccer, tennis, and basketball, but hockey was his first love. When he was six years old, his father took him to tryouts. "I didn't even have real skates," Hasek said. "I had those blades that you screw onto the soles of your shoes." The nine-year-old players didn't have a goaltender, and because Hasek was tall for his age, the league organizers put him with the older boys. Hasek quickly proved he had the skills to match his size.

Unlike their counterparts in the United States, young Czech goalies did not have coaches assigned to them to help sharpen their talents. Hasek had to learn to play on his own. "I would watch other goalies and try things they did," he said. "I'd say, 'Oh, this is good.' Or, 'Oh, this is not for me.'" Free to do as he pleased, Hasek developed the floppy, flapping style that is now his trademark.

Great athletes rely on training and practice to succeed, but the true stars also have special gifts that can't be taught. Even as a youngster in Pardubice, Hasek showed the amazing flexibility that has led to his success. He could do a leg split while on his knees, a move that startled his family doctor. And his legs weren't the only rubbery part of his body. One day Hasek's coach walked into the locker room and saw that his young goalie had, on a dare, stuffed his entire right hand into his mouth. The stunned coach thought to himself, "What if he can't take that hand back out?"

The hand did come out, and Hasek continued his excellent play, impressing everyone who saw him. In 1981 Zdenek Uher, the coach of Tesla Pardubice, needed a goaltender. Hasek, just 16 years old, was playing for the Tesla juniors, who were on their way to winning the national championship—in large part because of Hasek. Uher plucked Hasek from the junior team and made him goalie for the Tesla seniors. In his first full game in the top Czech league, Hasek helped Tesla to a 5–1 win.

Despite his talent and intelligence, Hasek sometimes gave Coach Uher fits. Like an absentminded professor, the goalie had a way of forgetting things. Before one big road game, Hasek left his equipment in Pardubice. He had to borrow small, well-worn pads from the home team. But the pads didn't affect Hasek's game, and Pardubice won 2–1. Said Frank Musil, an NHL defenseman and one of Hasek's teammates at the time, "He was the best player on the ice."

While playing for the national junior team, Hasek was almost fanatical about improving his game. After practice, he would challenge his teammates to try to beat him one-on-one. "I'll give you ten chances," he would dare. "Ten breakaways. See if you can beat me." If someone did score two or three times, Hasek wanted to do it over again.

Hasek's determination paid off. In his second season with the Tesla seniors, Hasek was the starting goalie, a position he kept for seven seasons. Tesla won two Czech national championships during that time, as Hasek gave up an average of fewer than three goals per game.

In 1983 the National Hockey League showed its first interest in the young Czech goalie with the unusual style. The Chicago Blackhawks chose Hasek as the 199th player in the Entry Draft. "I always secretly hoped that I'd come to the NHL, even when I was still a kid in Pardubice," Hasek later said. But at the time, just 18 years old, Hasek didn't know anything about the draft, and he didn't hear about his selection by the Blackhawks until a year later. Not that it would have mattered if he had.

At the time, Czechoslovakia was still a communist country under the sway of the Soviet Union. Czech citizens lacked freedom of speech and the ability to travel where they wished. In the 1950s Hasek's grandfather had been thrown in prison for opposing communist rule. In 1968, when Hasek was three years old, a new Czech government had tried to create a more open society, but the Soviet Union crushed the attempt, sending tanks into Prague. Not much had changed by 1983. Athletes were treated better than the average citizen, but as one friend of Hasek's said, "They even put hockey players in prison, you know."

The only way a Czech player could go to North America to play hockey was to defect, or leave illegally, without government permission. Defectors ran the risk of never seeing their friends and families again, and those loved ones left behind could be harassed by the police. Still, by this time a few players from Czechoslovakia had defected; the most famous were the Stastny brothers, Anton and Peter. Playing for the Quebec Nordiques, Peter was one of the top scorers in the NHL.

Hasek, still a teenager, was not about to defect. He wanted to go to college, and his life was fairly comfortable, though not luxurious. Besides, his career in Czechoslovakia was still on the rise. In 1984 he played for Czechoslovakia in the Canada Cup, an international competition featuring NHL players. Two years later he played on the national team in the World Hockey Championships and won the first of five consecutive awards as the best goalie in Czechoslovakia. At the 1987 World Championships, he was named the best goalie in the competition. That year he was also named Czechoslovakia's Player of the Year. Hockey experts agreed that Hasek was easily the best goalie in Europe.

By now the Chicago Blackhawks knew they had the rights to a hot property. The only problem was getting him to the United States. At the 1987 World Championships, the Blackhawks finally met with Hasek and offered him a contract: $1 million for five years. Hasek, still unwilling to defect, turned down the offer. He wanted to finish college and get his degree in history. And he liked his life in Pardubice. "I had a car," he said later. "I could order anything I wanted in any restaurant I want-

Hasek in October 1983, age 18, makes a save for Czechoslovakia's team in a match against Finland.

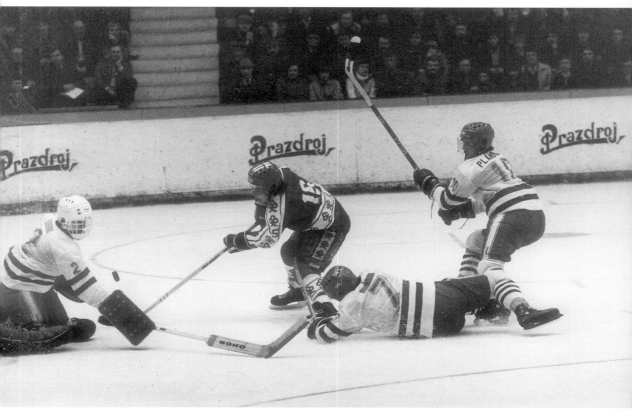

Hasek looks disappointed after a Czech loss to the Soviet Union in the 1987 World Championships. Yet he was named the best goalie in the competition, and the Chicago Black- hawks offered him a $1-million contract— which he turned down.

ed, people recognized me on the street. . . . I was happy."

After representing his homeland in the 1988 Olympics, Hasek finished his last season in Par- dubice. He owed a year of service to the Czech mil- itary, and in the 1989–90 season he played 40 games for his army team. As always, he played well, finishing with a 2.13 goals-against average (GAA). But his season ended on a sour note, as Hasek defied team orders and earned a six-game suspension.

Hasek's army club was facing his former team, Tesla, which was struggling without its star goalie. Tesla was in danger of finishing in last place, and if this happened, the team would be bumped down to a lower division for the following season. Hasek didn't want to beat his old team, so he told his coach he didn't want to play. The coach ordered him into goal anyway. About 20 seconds into the game, an angry Hasek skated off the ice and headed into the locker room. This behavior led to his suspension.

Hasek later said he had wanted to help Tesla stay in the upper division in part because he might return to the club the next season. But 1990 was the last year Hasek played a full season of hockey in Czechoslovakia. Late in 1989, democracy had finally come to the country. Hundreds of thousands of Czechs had marched in the streets of Prague, demanding an end to communist rule. This time, the people got their wish, and as a side effect of this momentous political change, Hasek was finally free to play hockey in North America.

His secret childhood dream of playing in the NHL was about to come true.

COMING TO AMERICA

As the 1990–91 season began, Dominik Hasek found himself in an unfamiliar position: the hero of Czech hockey was now a 25-year-old rookie in a foreign country.

Although the Chicago Blackhawks had been after him for seven years, Hasek had to earn a spot on the team's roster. The starting goaltending job seemed firmly in the hands of Ed Belfour. Just 25 himself, Belfour had played exceptionally well in the 1990 playoffs, with a 2.49 GAA in nine games.

Making things even tougher, Mike Keenan, the Blackhawks coach, had noticed a flaw in Hasek's game—his difficulty in handling the puck. Hasek had one more problem—he couldn't speak English. Goalies need to communicate quickly with their defensemen as they keep track of the puck. The Blackhawks decided the best way to help Hasek learn English and improve his play was to

In his second year in the NHL, Hasek makes a save against Pittsburgh's great Mario Lemieux in the Stanley Cup finals.

send him to the Indianapolis Ice, their farm team in the International Hockey League (IHL).

The move to the minors was productive. Hasek studied his new language and honed his skills with the stick. By this time, he had more than himself to think about: he had a wife, Alena, and a son, Michael. His success or failure on the ice would affect them as well.

Hasek played well in Indianapolis, and in November the Blackhawks brought him up to the big leagues. In his pro debut on November 6, 1990, he held the Hartford Whalers to a single goal in a 1–1 overtime tie. After the game, Keenan praised his rookie goalie's performance: "He had to make a lot of key saves for us, and there's no question about it, he's the reason we came out of here with a point tonight."

Despite that glowing review, Hasek was soon back in Indianapolis. For the year, Hasek played in 33 games for the Ice, compiling a 20–11–1 record. He led the league with five shutouts and a 2.52 GAA, earning a spot on the IHL All-Star Team.

Toward the end of the season, Hasek returned to the Blackhawks, where he earned his first NHL victory on March 8 against the Buffalo Sabres. He played in three more games that year, finishing with a 3–0–1 record and a fine 2.46 GAA. But considering the year Ed Belfour had had, it seemed unlikely that Hasek would earn more playing time the following season. Belfour won Rookie of the Year honors and the Vezina Trophy, awarded to the league's best goalie. He also took the Jennings Trophy, which goes to one or more goalies on the team that compiles the lowest goals-against average.

As the 1991–92 season started, Hasek felt dis-

Hasek's early years in the NHL were a learning experience. Here he gives up a goal to Adam Graves of the New York Rangers.

couraged. When he was sent back to Indianapolis in November, his confidence began to slide. Sometimes he took the ice and didn't care if he played well. "There was one incredible game," Hasek said, "where they scored on me nine times. I'd never been through anything like that before." Finally, in January 1992, Keenan called Hasek back to Chicago.

Once again, when given the chance to play for the Blackhawks, Hasek responded well. He had learned from watching Belfour to be more aggressive, to leave the crease to challenge shooters or to chase down the puck. On the larger rinks in Czechoslovakia, such roaming could be fatal, but in Chicago it became a more important part of Hasek's game.

June 1, 1992, last game of the Stanley Cup finals: Hasek experiences the privilege of playing in a championship game—and the pain of giving up the series-clinching goal to the Pittsburgh Penguins.

During that second year in the NHL, Hasek played in 20 regular-season games, finishing with a 10–4–1 record and a 2.60 GAA. In the playoffs he was in goal for three games during the Black-hawks' unsuccessful run at the Stanley Cup. He was selected for the league's All-Rookie Team. But despite his quality play, Hasek was not part of the Blackhawks' long-range plans. In August he was traded to the Buffalo Sabres for goalie Stephane Beauregard and a future draft pick.

Moving to Buffalo renewed Hasek's optimism.

He made his Sabres debut on opening day, and he achieved his first win for the Sabres on October 23. But just as Hasek felt he had found his groove in Buffalo, he was injured. He sat out almost a month. When he was ready to return in late February, he was jolted with more bad news: the Sabres had traded for Grant Fuhr, one of the top netminders in the league. Once again Hasek was relegated to a backup role.

Although he spent the whole 1992–93 season in the NHL, Hasek played in just 28 games. His record was 11–10–4, and his GAA rose to 3.15. In the playoffs, the Sabres reached the second round, where they lost four straight to the Montreal Canadiens. In eight playoff games, Hasek made just one appearance.

In the off-season, Hasek signed a new contract worth $400,000 a year—a good salary for a backup goalie. The contract also included bonuses if Hasek made the All-Star Team or if he won the Vezina Trophy—unlikely events, it appeared at the time. "It all seemed so ridiculous for a backup goalie back then," Hasek said, "but [my agent] thought those ridiculous clauses were good to have just in case."

As it turned out, the agent proved wiser than anyone had suspected.

FINALLY NUMBER ONE

In 1992–93, the Buffalo Sabres had finished fourth in their division, winning just two games more than they lost. The team had two high scorers, Alexander Mogilny and former Olympian Pat LaFontaine. Mogilny had scored 76 goals, tied for best in the league, while LaFontaine was the league's second-best overall scorer, with 148 points. With that potent offensive duo and solid goaltending from Grant Fuhr and Dominik Hasek, the Sabres hoped to improve their record in 1993–94.

Before the season began, and before he signed his new contract, Hasek almost ended up playing for another NHL team. The league added two new teams that year, the Florida Panthers and the Mighty Ducks of Anaheim. The new teams were allowed to pick players from the existing teams in an expansion draft. The Sabres protected two goalies from the draft, and Hasek wasn't one of them. But neither expansion club picked him.

In the 1993–94 season Hasek emerged as the Sabres' starting goalie—and the best in the NHL.

Early in the season, the Sabres realized how lucky they were not to have lost Hasek in the draft. In November, Fuhr went out of the lineup with a knee injury. LaFontaine was already out for the rest of the season after knee surgery. The Sabres needed a spark if they were going to have a chance at the playoffs, and Hasek provided it.

Starting in late November, Hasek played in 29 straight games. But he didn't just fill the goal crease, he dominated it, diving and falling and sprawling to make save after save. Between November 26 and December 31, he gave up more than two goals in only two games. On November 29 he recorded a 3–0 shutout over the Toronto Maple Leafs, his first shutout with the Sabres. The next game, Hasek faced 33 shots and shut down the Florida Panthers by the same score. Another 3–0 shutout came in Hartford two weeks later. By that point, Hasek had given up scarcely one goal per game in the nine times he had started in place of Fuhr.

Opposing players were still shaking their heads over Hasek's unorthodox style, but Sabres coach John Muckler wasn't concerned. "What is the right way and the wrong way to play goal?" asked Muckler. "All I know is the guy stops the puck. How can you argue with success?"

The Sabres and their fans weren't arguing. The team was on a roll, and Hasek was leading the league in goaltending. His overall average was under two goals per game, and he was stopping about 93 percent of the shots taken at him. He finished the month of December with five shutouts and was named the NHL's co-Player of the Month.

In the last game of that month, on December 31, Hasek faced the New York Rangers. Led by Mark Messier and Brian Leetch, the Rangers were playing well and were on their way to their first Stanley Cup championship in 54 years. Behind the bench was Hasek's former coach in Chicago, Mike Keenan. Hasek might have found some extra pleasure in that game, since he allowed Keenan's team just one goal on 40 shots as the Sabres won, 4–1. During one particularly brilliant stretch, as New York skated with a two-man power-play advantage, Hasek stopped 8 shots. After the game Keenan said, "He's an outstanding goaltender.

"What is the right way and the wrong way to play goal?" asked Hasek's coach, John Muckler. Here, against Brian Noonan of the New York Rangers, the unorthodox Hasek showed he would go to any lengths to stop a potential score.

That was the name of the game tonight—Dominik Hasek."

In February Fuhr returned to the lineup, but Hasek was still at top form and kept his position as the Sabres' number-one goalie. "Grant and I have been through a lot of wars together," Muckler said, "and he's been very important to my own success. But Dominik is clearly the best goalie in the NHL at this time."

Fuhr, though frustrated first by his injury and then by losing his starting job, appreciated Hasek's great play as well. "It wasn't fun sitting on the bench," he said, "but it was fun watching Dominik stone every opponent he faced. Most people would say Ron Hextall is the most fiery competitor they've ever seen in goal, but I would disagree. I think it's Dominik Hasek."

By the time the regular season ended, Hasek compiled a record of 30 wins, 20 losses, and 6 ties. He notched 7 shutouts, tied for best in the league, and his .930 save percentage led the league. Most amazing of all, he kept his goals-against average below 2.00, finishing at 1.95. Hasek was the first goalie to break the magic mark of 2.00 since the 1973–74 season, when Philadelphia Flyers goalie and Hall-of-Famer Bernie Parent registered a 1.89 GAA. During the entire season, Hasek played just four games in which he allowed more than three goals—and two of those were overtime games.

Hasek's numbers were the visible proof of the confidence he felt. "I believed all the time I could be among the best NHL goalies," he said. "That's why I came to play in the NHL. I always knew I could be one of the best. But you cannot prove it if you sit on the bench."

The Sabres finished the 1993–94 regular season with 95 points, a 9-point improvement over the previous season, and much of the gain was the result of Hasek's play. Now, in the playoffs, Buffalo would face the New Jersey Devils, the team with the second-best record in the league. The Devils had their own hot goalie, Martin Brodeur. Just 21, Brodeur won the Calder Trophy that year as the NHL's Rookie of the Year.

The playoff series seesawed back and forth, with Hasek shutting out the Devils in the first game, then New Jersey winning the next two. Buffalo won the fourth game, 5–3, then lost the next by the identical score. The Sabres had to win Game 6 to avoid elimination. Luckily, Hasek was at his best during what turned out to be a historic game.

Both Hasek and Brodeur were sharp, stopping every shot they faced. On one play in the first period, Hasek made a save while lying on his back—not textbook goaltending, but typical for him. Later, with just under six minutes to play in the game, Hasek made another fine save, sliding across the crease to stop a two-on-one breakaway. Along the way, the Sabres thought they had scored three separate times, but each goal was waved off for different reasons by the referee. After 60 minutes of regulation play, the two teams were locked in a scoreless tie.

Despite the usual tension in a playoff overtime, Hasek and Brodeur somehow stayed perfect. One overtime period passed. Then another. And another. The two teams had played the equivalent of two scoreless games in one night. Finally, 5 minutes and 43 seconds into the fourth overtime, more than 6 hours after the game had started, the Sabres' Dave Hannan flipped a backhand shot

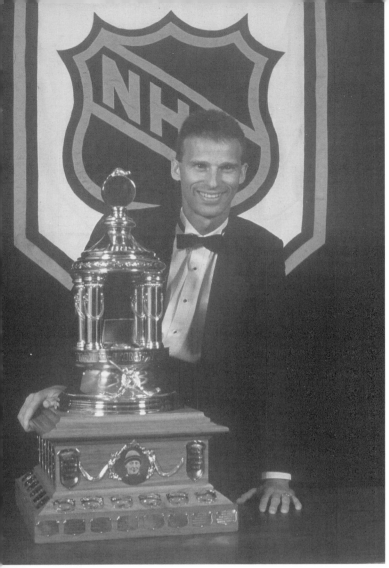

Sweet recognition: Hasek with the 1994 Vezina Trophy, awarded to the top goaltender in the NHL.

over a sprawled Brodeur to earn a 1–0 victory. In the sixth-longest playoff game in NHL history, Buffalo had evened the series.

In more than 120 minutes of hockey, Hasek had stopped an amazing 70 shots. Veteran Devils center Bob Carpenter said, "I thought Hasek played the best game I ever saw a goalie play. I thought we had a lot better chances to score than they did." Yet Hasek made it sound like his performance was not so impressive. "The players get more tired than I do," he said. "The shots in overtime are not so hard. Many come from the blue line. Maybe it's easier for the goalie."

In the deciding game of the series, Hasek once again faced a barrage of shots, stopping 42 of 44 scoring chances. But this time Brodeur and the Devils were just a little bit better—the Sabres could get only one shot past the rookie netminder. Although the Sabres went home disappointed, Hasek finished the series with a 1.61 GAA, a sparkling end to a remarkable season.

In June, when the NHL gave out its annual awards, Hasek collected the Vezina Trophy as the best goalie. He also shared with Grant Fuhr the Jennings Trophy for the fewest goals allowed per game. Another honor for Hasek was being named a first-team All-Star. A number of sports publications also named him to their all-star teams, and he finished second in the voting for the NHL's Hart Trophy, given to the league's Most Valuable Player. In just one season, Hasek had gone from back-up goalie to one of the league's top stars.

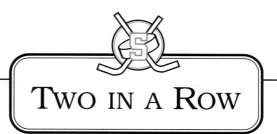

After his success in 1993–94, Dominik Hasek was eager to get back on the ice the following year. But before the season started, he went to the Sabres' management to discuss signing a new contract. A superstar goalie deserved to be paid like a superstar, he felt. When the Sabres seemed reluctant, Hasek sat out a week of training camp, determined to get what he was worth. Before the end of September, he had a new contract that would pay him $7 million for the next three seasons.

Another obstacle then delayed Hasek and the rest of the Sabres from starting the 1994–95 season: the NHL owners and players were caught in a labor dispute about salary limits. The owners refused to begin another season without an agreement, and they locked the players out of the arenas. Opening day came and went without a resolution.

While the negotiations continued, Hasek tried to stay in shape on his own. As the labor dispute

The large contract Hasek signed in 1994 did not change his sprawling style of play.

dragged on through November and December, Hasek spent some time back in the Czech Republic. He even donned his pads to play two games with Pardubice. Finally, the players and owners reached an agreement. The Sabres opened their season on January 20 against the Stanley Cup champions, the New York Rangers. But in a surprise move, Grant Fuhr, not Hasek, was in goal.

Fuhr and the Sabres won, 2–1, but Hasek didn't have to worry about competing for the starting goalie job again. The Sabres were paying him too much to keep him on the bench. A few weeks later, Fuhr was traded to the Los Angeles Kings, and Hasek ended up playing in 41 of Buffalo's 48 games during the shortened season. By this time, his spectacular play had earned Hasek a nickname—the Dominator—and once again he was one of the league's top goalies.

He finished the regular season with 19 wins, fifth best in the league. And he did it without much offensive support from his teammates. In 15 games, the Sabres had scored two or fewer goals, but Hasek still managed to win or tie 10 of them. The Sabres scored just 130 goals for the season—only one other team that made the playoffs had fewer. Hasek, though, never complained about the Sabres' lack of firepower; he even seemed to welcome the challenge it presented. "When games are low scoring, when they're close, I find it more exciting," he said. "When you're able to make big saves at the end of a game, it's a great feeling."

Hasek made plenty of big saves that year. His 2.11 GAA was tied for best in the league, and he also shared the lead in shutouts with five. For the second straight year, he led all goalies in save percentage, stopping .930 of the shots he faced. He ended the season with two shutouts in his last four games. The Sabres, however, finished in the middle of the standings, and entering the playoffs they were clear underdogs to the Atlantic Division champs, the Philadelphia Flyers.

The Flyers were led by high-scoring Eric Lindros, who centered a line known as the Legion of Doom. Lindros and wingers John LeClair and Mikael Renberg were all at least 6'2" and weighed more than 220 pounds. Their combination of speed and size made them one of the most feared offensive threesomes in the league. Lindros had given Hasek a taste of his toughness in a game two weeks before the playoffs. Putting his glove in the goalie's face, Lindros shoved him to the ice. Hasek ignored the play, and he and the Sabres beat the Flyers, 4–2.

Things did not go so well for the Sabres in the first playoff game. The Flyers were intent on using their superior size to clog up the crease and make it difficult for Hasek to follow the puck. In Game 1 Philadelphia played without Lindros, who had injured his eye, but they had plenty of other large bodies to throw in front of the net. The two teams skated to a 3–3 tie in regulation. About 10 minutes into overtime, Flyers defenseman Karl Dykhuis launched a bouncing, wobbly puck that slipped past Hasek, giving Philadelphia a 4–3 win.

Surrounded by Sabres teammates—Alexei Zhitnik behind him, Garry Galley and Jason Dawe nearby—Hasek cannot block the bouncing shot by Karl Dykhuis that scored the winning goal for the Flyers in Game 1 of the 1995 playoff series.

Trade rumors and injuries made 1995–96 a frustrating season for Hasek. The Sabres also missed the playoffs that year.

The second game was just as hard for Hasek and the Sabres. At one point in the second period, when LeClair planted himself in the crease and blocked Hasek's view, Hasek slammed the ice with his stick, seemingly frustrated by the situation. The Flyers won, 3–1. After the game, Sabres coach John Muckler said, "Their two big guys [LeClair and Renberg], especially, are hard to handle. . . . But I thought we did a much better job of protecting Dom than we did in the first game. Our problem is we just can't score."

Hasek was very sharp in Game 3 as the Sabres won, 3–1. He stopped 18 shots, and the only Flyers goal came on a power play. The next game, however, Eric Lindros was back from his injury, and he helped the Flyers take a 4–0 lead by the second period. The final score was 4–2. Hasek seemed just as shaky the next game, giving up four goals in the first period. Even though the Sabres managed to get back into the game, the Flyers won, 6–4, clinching the series.

Once again, the Sabres had made an early exit from the playoffs. Hasek, however, was again recognized for his fine play during the regular season. He won his second Vezina Trophy and was named to the NHL First All-Star Team.

During the off-season, Hasek's place on the Sabres' roster was in question, despite his great success. The team was struggling financially. It traded the high-scoring (and high-priced) Alexander Mogilny to Vancouver. *The Sporting News* reported rumors that the Sabres had been looking to trade Hasek as well. Muckler admitted the team was trying to redesign Hasek's contract in order to pay him less in the near term but keep him for a longer time and pay him more in the future. "We're looking at every possible way to keep

Hasek dives to the ice to stop a shot by the Tampa Bay Lightning's Brian Bradley (19) in December 1995. Despite his losing record that season, Hasek led the league in save percentage.

him," Muckler said. "We don't want to let the best goaltender in the game get away."

When the 1995–96 season started, Hasek was still in net for the Sabres. But the season turned out to be a disappointing one for him and the team. At one point a muscle strain in his stomach forced him to miss 10 games, and later he was bothered with a knee injury. For the first time in his NHL career, Hasek lost more games than he won, posting a 22–30–6 record. His goals-against average

rose to 2.83—still respectable for most goalies, but not up to the Dominator's usual standards. With Hasek off his game, the Sabres missed making the playoffs for the first time in almost a decade.

The season was not a total loss, however. Playing in the All-Star Game in Boston, Hasek helped the East beat the West, 5–4, stopping 12 of 13 shots during the one period he played. And he once again led the league in save percentage, with a .920 figure. His play was still dazzling enough to frustrate hockey's best shooters. In March he stopped the great Mario Lemieux of the Pittsburgh Penguins on a penalty shot, the toughest one-on-one challenge for any goalie.

The consensus was growing: the Dominator was one of the greatest goalies ever.

HIGHS AND LOWS

$\mathbf{A}$s he prepared for the 1996–97 season, Dominik Hasek sat down with the Sabres' general manager, John Muckler, to discuss a new contract. Muckler had moved from the bench to the front office in 1995, turning over the coaching duties to Ted Nolan. Muckler and Hasek agreed to another three-year deal, this one worth just over $12 million. Also in the contract was a no-trade clause. By now Hasek had a young daughter, Dominika, and his son, Michael, was truly Americanized. The family felt comfortable in upstate New York. "Buffalo is like a new home for me," Hasek said.

On the ice, however, the season did not promise to be a good one for the Sabres. Most hockey experts picked them to miss the playoffs once again. And, once again, bad luck struck the team early. Tension grew between Nolan and Muckler; at one point Nolan thought about quitting. Star

The 1996–97 season looked bleak for the Sabres until Hasek, shown here in a game against the Ottawa Senators, stepped up his play.

center Pat LaFontaine suffered a severe concussion in November, forcing him out for the season. Days after, the giant scoreboard in the Sabres' new Marine Midland Arena crashed to the ice. Luckily, none of the players were on the rink at the time, but the mishap looked like an omen. The Sabres seemed doomed to a hopeless season.

But starting in mid-November, Hasek stepped up his game, pulling the Sabres out of their slump. On November 14 the Sabres beat the defending Stanley Cup champions, the Colorado Avalanche, handing them their first loss in 12 games. That victory started a run that boosted the Sabres' prospects. Later in the month, Hasek had a 3–0 shutout against Tampa Bay, stopping 32 shots. Two nights later, he beat the Ottawa Senators by the same score. About two weeks later, he blanked the Boston Bruins, 4–0.

On December 23 the Sabres traveled to New Jersey for a game with the Devils. In a performance that brought to mind the marathon playoff game of 1994, Hasek and Martin Brodeur dueled to a 0–0 tie. Each goalie stopped 37 shots. Four of Hasek's saves came in overtime, including a last-second glove save that preserved the tie. When the Sabres later beat the Devils 6–5 on New Year's Eve, Buffalo finished a 13–6–2 stretch that had begun with the victory over the Avalanche.

The great play continued in 1997. Through January and February, the Sabres lost only five times. Everyone on the Sabres team, and around the league, knew Hasek was the key factor. Hasek enjoyed his role. "My teammates depend on me," he said. "That's the way it is. I like it." His coach was appreciative as well. "He is a Gretzky in net," said Ted Nolan. "He sees the shot the guy is going to take, two passes before he takes it."

By early March the division-leading Sabres had won 34 games; Hasek had been in net for 33 of them, and he led the league with a .927 save percentage. But just a week later, Hasek was on the bench, nursing a cracked rib. He suffered the injury on March 8 in a game against the Montreal Canadiens. Charging out to the blue line to track down a loose puck, Hasek collided with a Canadiens player. He tried to play with the pain, but had to take some time off. In the five games he missed, Buffalo lost four times.

Hasek returned to the ice on April 1 to face the New York Rangers. Wearing a special chest protector for his rib, Hasek stopped 37 shots in a 1–1 tie. He held the Rangers scoreless until 6:28 remained in the game, when left wing Esa Tikkanen beat him with a shorthanded goal off a rebound.

After that game, Tikkanen's teammate Wayne Gretzky joined the growing chorus of praise for Hasek. In the first period of the game, the Great One had skated in on a breakaway and unleashed a slapshot from the left faceoff circle. Hasek stopped it cold. Now Gretzky declared that Hasek was a top candidate for the MVP award: "It would be hard if you are voting not to vote for that guy."

Despite the losing streak before the Rangers game, the Sabres stayed on top in the Northeast Division. On April 10 they clinched their first division title in 16 years with a 5–1 victory over the Boston Bruins. It was Hasek's 37th win of the season, a personal best.

After the game, Hasek and his teammates celebrated their fine season. "If someone had asked me six months ago if we could win the division," he reflected, "I would have said it was impossible. But this is a young team that has grown together and gained confidence, and now we are the winners."

In the first round of the playoffs, the Sabres faced the Ottawa Senators, who were making their first postseason appearance. Ottawa was led by a trio of young stars, Alexei Yashin, Alexandre Daigle, and Daniel Alfredsson. In net the Senators had veteran goalie Ron Tugnutt.

Given Hasek's hot play and the Senators' lack of experience, the Sabres were favored to win. They took the first game easily, 3–1. But in the second game Hasek had some problems, the prologue to one of the worst periods in his professional career.

In that game the Senators beat the Sabres, 3–1, and each goal came off a rebound. Normally Hasek is a master at controlling rebounds and denying his opponents a second shot. He either deflects a shot into one of the corners, far from the net, or pounces on the rebound to force a faceoff. But not in this game.

Afterward, Hasek's performance seemed to bother him. He played poorly in the team's next practice. The day of Game 3, he missed a team meeting and skipped an optional workout—unusual for him. In warm-ups, shots seemed to whistle by him. He smacked his stick in frustration and skated out of the crease; his teammates had to encourage him to return. As this went on, the Ottawa fans in the arena taunted him.

When the game began, Hasek held Ottawa scoreless for the first period. In the second, while trying to stop a power-play goal, Hasek sprained his right knee. He left the game, which the Sabres eventually won, and sat on the bench with his teammates. Hasek didn't seem to be in a lot of pain—he wasn't on crutches and didn't ice his knee.

Back on the ice after his rib injury, Hasek makes a save in April 1997 against Alexandre Daigle of the Ottawa Senators. But in the playoffs that year Hasek was haunted by injury and public controversy.

After the game he stayed with an old friend from Pardubice, Frank Musil, who now played for the Senators. Some people, including his teammates, found it odd that Hasek would stay with his play-off "enemy." "Dominik just wanted some quiet time," explained Musil. "He was very disappoint-ed in his injury."

The Sabres were disappointed too, as were their fans and the sportswriters who followed the team. Jim Kelley of *The Buffalo News* suggested that something else was wrong with Hasek, not just his injured knee: "I do believe the pressure of having to be unbeatable may well be more than even he can bear." The tone of the article seemed to question Hasek's recent actions and his commitment to his team in the playoffs. A few days later, an angry Hasek grabbed the writer in the Marine Midland Arena in a confrontation that resulted in the writer's shirt being torn. Hasek later apologized, but the league suspended him for three games.

Mitch Korn, the Sabres' goalie coach, defended Hasek throughout the ordeal. "Dom was hurt, plain and simple," Korn said. "He knows his body very well. Some of the things that were written and said were so ludicrous. It was absolutely insane. He couldn't play, and for people to question that is unbelievable." Hasek, however, wanted to hear a public defense from head coach Ted Nolan as well. When it didn't come, the relationship between the coach and the superstar grew strained.

The Sabres managed to beat Ottawa without Hasek, but playing the Philadelphia Flyers in the second round was another story. The Flyers held a 2–1 edge after the first three games. Hasek could have played in Games 4 and 5, but Nolan stayed with backup goalie Steve Shields. The Flyers won the series, 4–1.

The controversy of the playoffs faded a bit in June, when the NHL announced its awards for the season. Not surprisingly, Hasek won his third Vezina Trophy. He had once again led the league in save percentage, at .930, and tied for second in wins. His goals-against average, 2.27, was fourth best. Hasek also became the first goalie in 35 years to win the Hart Trophy, given to the Most Valuable Player as selected by the journalists who cover the NHL. Finally, he took the Lester Pearson Award, given to the league's top player as voted by the other players.

During the summer, there was more grumbling in Buffalo. Hasek and Nolan had not been on the best of terms all season, and the incident with Jim Kelley made things worse. Hasek told reporters he thought the team would be better off with a new coach. He believed Nolan did not treat the European-born players well. The Sabres' management took the hint and fired Nolan, replacing him with a former Buffalo player, Lindy Ruff.

Some Sabres, such as the hard-nosed winger Matthew Barnaby, liked Nolan. Barnaby resented Hasek's role in Nolan's departure. It was widely reported that Barnaby threatened to dump Hasek to the ice the first chance he had during the fall training camp.

Hasek didn't seem concerned. He spent time in the Czech Republic, and then came back ready to put the problems of the spring behind him. He wanted to focus on proving that he had earned his awards and all the praise as the best goalie in the NHL.

STILL
NUMBER ONE

When the Sabres' training camp opened in September 1997, anyone who expected fireworks had to be disappointed. Despite Matthew Barnaby's heated criticism of Dominik Hasek concerning the Ted Nolan firing, everything was quiet. The two players met to discuss their differences and said the incident was over.

The Buffalo fans, however, were not so quick to forget. They booed Hasek in preseason competition and again at the team's home opener of the regular season. Hasek had never been booed before. He tried to shrug off the fans' angry response, but later he admitted that the booing had stung him, and it seemed to affect his play.

On October 19 he was pulled from the game after two periods of a 5–2 loss to Chicago. In a mid-November game against the Edmonton Oilers, Hasek let in three goals on just nine shots. The Sabres, defending Northeast Division champs,

The masked man grins as he returns to the Sabres in March 1998 after leading the Czech Republic to an Olympic gold medal.

53

were in last place. They had not won a home game with Hasek in net. The team's other superstar, Pat LaFontaine, had left in the off-season, so the Sabres had even fewer offensive weapons than in the past. With Hasek off his form, the team was in trouble.

Before a game with the Washington Capitals, Coach Lindy Ruff told Hasek that backup goalie Steve Shields was going to start, and that Shields would remain in net if he stayed hot. The Dominator was being benched. Hasek tried to be understanding about the demotion. "You do not play well, and the other goalie gets a start," he said. "I will work hard in practice. I will get my confidence back."

The turning point came at the end of November, when the Sabres hosted the New York Rangers, LaFontaine's new team. The Buffalo fans cheered him while taunting Hasek. The two teams played to a 3–3 tie. Afterward, fans waited outside the arena to throw more harsh words at Hasek. "Dom changed after that night," said Sabres general manager Darcy Regier. "He realized he couldn't listen to what people said, and he couldn't control the crowd. He could only control the game. He became totally focused."

The next week, the Sabres played four games. Against the Philadelphia Flyers, the Sabres managed a 1–1 tie. In the next two games, against Anaheim and Tampa Bay, Hasek recorded identical 4–0 shutouts. He finished the week with a 2–1–1 record. His GAA for that week was 0.74, and his save percentage a startling .974. That performance earned him Player of the Week honors. Hasek gave credit to his teammates for playing better defensively. He also said he felt more support from the

Buffalo fans. Whatever the reason, Hasek's confidence had definitely returned.

Through December, Hasek remained the hottest goalie in the league. He shut out the Montreal Canadiens, 1–0, then blanked the Rangers twice in five days. On New Year's Eve he recorded his sixth shutout of the month, a 3–0 win over the Ottawa Senators. With that game Hasek set a

Greg Adams of the Dallas Stars scores against Hasek on October 7, 1997. Booed by the fans, Hasek struggled early in the season.

record for most shutouts in a month during hockey's "modern" era, which dates from 1929.

In January Hasek played in his third consecutive All-Star Game. In the skills contest before the game, he won the breakaway competition, stopping such high scorers as Wayne Gretzky, Mark Recchi, and Mike Modano one-on-one. That performance was an early sign of what would follow when Hasek and the Czech team went to Nagano, Japan, for the Olympics. Hasek's performance in leading the Czechs to the gold medal won him more international fame than ever.

When Hasek returned from Nagano, he was greeted by 500 fans at the Buffalo airport. Reporters descended on him as well, trying to interview the man many were calling "the greatest goaltender in the world." Some even suggested he was the greatest player in the game.

The Dominator prepares to knock down a shot in Game 4 of the Sabres' 1998 playoff series against the Philadelphia Flyers. In Games 3 and 4 alone, Hasek blocked 75 of 77 shots on goal.

As the NHL season resumed after the Olympics, Hasek and the Sabres continued their hot play. In his first three games, Hasek had two shutouts, and by the end of March he added three more. After a 1–0 win over the Edmonton Oilers, Sabres left wing Geoff Sanderson spoke of the "luxury" of having to score only one goal to win. "It's happened so many times this year—we only score one goal, and Dom shuts the door." A few days later, Hasek provided that luxury again, getting his 13th and final shutout of the season in a 4–0 win over the Los Angeles Kings. No goalie had recorded so many shutouts in one year since 1953–54.

The Sabres had managed to overcome their slow start and put together a winning record: 36–29–17. After January 1, they were the best team in the NHL, despite a less-than-potent offense. Of the team's three top scorers—Miroslav Satan, Alexei Zhitnik, and Donald Audette—none had more than 50 points or 25 goals. As in the past, the defense, led by Hasek, was the difference. His personal numbers were even better than they had been the previous year. His GAA fell to 2.09, while his save percentage inched up to .932—once again the best in the league. The Sabres entered the playoffs with confidence, believing they had the hottest goalie in the world.

In the first round the Sabres faced the Philadelphia Flyers, a great offensive team that had reached the Stanley Cup finals the year before. The Sabres would have to rely on their quickness—and on Hasek. The Sabres got off to a good start, taking the first game 3–2. The Flyers came back in Game 2, winning 3–2 on a power-play goal by John LeClair. In Game 3 the Sabres showed some unusual firepower, winning 6–1; Hasek's bid for a shutout ended with just 6:09 left in the game.

In Game 4 Hasek once again had a shutout going into the third period. The game ended with the Sabres on top, 4–1. In the last two games Hasek had stopped 75 of 77 shots.

In Game 5 Hasek and Flyers goalie Sean Burke both played well; after regulation the game was tied at 2. Then, almost six minutes into overtime, the Sabres' Michal Grosek scored on a power play. The Sabres took the series—their first playoff series win since Hasek had joined the team.

Next up for the Sabres were the Montreal Canadiens. No one would confuse this Montreal team with the powerhouse champions of old, but they had such stars as Mark Recchi, Andy Moog, and Vincent Damphousse. Game 1 was a tight match, with the Canadiens outplaying the Sabres for much of the game. In overtime, however, Hasek was perfect, and a Geoff Sanderson goal gave the Sabres a 3–2 win. In Game 2 Hasek gave up three goals before the end of the second period. The Sabres tied the score; then Matthew Barnaby went on a scoring tear, putting in three straight goals for his first career hat trick. The Sabres headed to Montreal with a comfortable 2–0 lead in the series.

In Game 3 Hasek once again got off to a shaky start. He gave up two goals on the Canadiens' first three shots, and four through the first two periods. Montreal goalie Jocelyn Thibault was having just as much trouble—he gave up four goals on 13 shots. The score remained tied through regulation. After the two teams played one scoreless overtime period, Michael Peca scored in the second overtime to give the Sabres the win. Once again, Hasek had saved his best performance for the pressure situation, stopping 28 shots in the last half of the game.

The Sabres now had a commanding 3–0 series lead. In Game 4 the Sabres scored first on a power play after Canadiens defenseman Dave Manson was penalized for slashing Hasek. Throughout the series, Montreal had tried to rattle Hasek with rough play, but each time the tactic had led to a penalty and a Sabres score. In this game the Canadiens scored in the second period, but it was the only goal Hasek allowed. With a 3–1 victory, Buffalo swept the series and headed to the Eastern Conference finals for the first time in 18 years.

In the four games against the Canadiens, Hasek had a .940 save percentage, allowing just 10 goals on 158 shots. Canadiens forward Mark Recchi thought Hasek had made the difference for the Sabres. "I hope every one of them tucks in every night and says thank you [for Hasek]," Recchi declared. "He's incredible."

Hasek didn't have much time to savor the victory, since he was about to face the hottest goalie in the playoffs, Olaf Kolzig of the Washington Capitals. In Washington's previous round against the Ottawa Senators, Kolzig had recorded back-to-back shutouts, and he had a total of three at this point in the postseason.

In Game 1 it was Hasek's turn to notch the shutout, as he stopped 19 shots and the Sabres won, 2–0. The next few games, however, were much tougher. Washington won Game 2 in overtime by a 3–2 score when Todd Krygier beat Hasek with a high shot on his glove side. In the next game, Peter Bondra unleashed an overtime slapshot that gave the Capitals a 4–3 win. They built a commanding 3–1 series lead with Game 4, a 2–0 shutout for Kolzig. In a play that silenced the crowd at Marine Midland Arena, Hasek failed to stop Joe Juneau's shorthanded shot from just across the center line. "Probably the first time in my life I let in a goal from past the blue line," Hasek said afterward. "It's disappointing, but sometimes it happens."

After that fluke goal, and with his team facing elimination, Hasek decided to do something different. To break the tension and poke fun at himself, the goalie put a piece of tape over his name on the back of his practice jersey. On the tape he wrote "Swiss Cheese," since he had been so full of holes the past few games. But there was nothing cheesy about his performance in Game 5. In another brilliant game, he stopped 34 shots as the Sabres won, 2–1. "I made some saves I didn't even know how I made," he said afterward. "Sometimes the bounces don't go my way. Today I was more lucky."

The Sabres' and Hasek's luck, however, ran out the next game. Playing in front of a home crowd, Hasek gave up a game-winning overtime goal to Caps center Joe Juneau. The series, and an amazing year, were over.

Hasek wouldn't win a Stanley Cup championship ring to go with his gold medal—not this year. But he did add some individual trophies to his collection, sweeping the top two awards—the Vezina Trophy for goaltending and the Hart Trophy as Most Valuable Player—for the second year in a row. And the Buffalo Sabres, the youngest team in the NHL, seemed poised to contend for the Cup again. It's hard to count out any team that has Dominik Hasek standing—or sitting, or sprawling—in the net.

STATISTICS

Season	Team	Regular Season						Playoffs				
		GP	W	L	T	GAA	SPCT	GP	W	L	GAA	SPCT
1990–91	Chi	5	3	0	1	2.46	.914	3	0	0	2.61	.923
1991–92	Chi	20	10	4	1	2.60	.893	3	0	2	3.04	.886
1992–93	Buf	28	11	10	4	3.15	.896	1	1	0	1.33	.957
1993–94	Buf	58	30	20	6	1.95	.930	7	3	4	1.61	.950
1994–95	Buf	41	19	14	7	2.11	.930	5	1	4	3.50	.863
1995–96	Buf	59	22	30	6	2.83	.920	—	—	—	—	—
1996–97	Buf	67	37	20	10	2.27	.930	3	1	1	1.96	.926
1997–98	Buf	72	33	23	13	2.09	.932	15	10	5	2.03	.938
Totals		350	165	121	48	2.34	.924	37	16	16	2.22	.928

GP   games played
W   wins
L   losses
T   ties
GAA   goals-against average
SPCT save percentage

CHRONOLOGY

1965   Dominik Hasek is born on January 29 in Pardubice, Czechoslovakia.

1990   Hasek is signed by the Chicago Blackhawks of the National Hockey League after a successful career in Czechoslovakia, where he was named the country's best player in 1987, 1989, and 1990.

1990–91   Makes his debut with the Blackhawks, but spends most of the season in the minors.

1992   Named to the NHL All-Rookie Team after finishing the year with a 10–4–1 record and a 2.60 goals-against average (GAA); during the off-season, he is traded to the Buffalo Sabres.

1993   As a backup goalie, finishes the 1992–93 season with a record of 11–10–4; in November, takes over for Grant Fuhr as the Sabres' starting goalie.

1994   Wins the Vezina Trophy after leading the league with a 1.95 GAA and a .930 save percentage; becomes the first NHL goaltender in 20 years to finish with a GAA below 2.00; named the NHL's first-team All-Star goalie.

1995   Again wins the Vezina and leads the league in save percentage (.930), tying for the lead in GAA (2.11); again named the league's first-team All-Star goalie; finishes second in the voting for Most Valuable Player.

1996   Plays in his first All-Star Game and stops 12 of 13 shots; leads the league in save percentage for third consecutive year (.920); signs a long-term contract with the Sabres worth more than $12 million.

1997   The Sabres win their first division championship in 16 years, thanks largely to Hasek; for the 1996–97 season he posts a 37–20–10 record with a 2.27 GAA; his .930 save percentage once again leads the league; wins his third Vezina Trophy and becomes the first goalie in 35 years to win the Hart Trophy for Most Valuable Player.

1998   Helps the Czech Republic win the gold medal at the winter Olympics in Nagano, Japan, stopping 148 of 154 shots in six games; finishes the NHL regular season with a record of 33–23–13 with 13 shutouts, best in the league; his .932 save percentage is a career high and once again leads the league; wins the Hart Trophy as Most Valuable Player for the second straight year, and the Vezina Trophy as the top goalie for the fourth time in five years.

FURTHER READING

Brodeur, Denis, and Daniel Daignault. *Goalies: Guardians of the Net.* Toronto: Key Parks, 1995.

Fischler, Stan, and Chico Resch. *Hot Goalies.* Toronto: Warwick, 1997.

The National Hockey League Official Guide and Record Book, 1997–98. Chicago: Triumph, 1997.

Novak, Jan. "Leaving the Net." *Men's Journal,* December 1994–January 1995.

The Sporting News Hockey Guide, 1997–98. St. Louis: The Sporting News, 1997.

ABOUT THE AUTHOR

Michael Burgan has written more than 20 books for children and young adults, both fiction and nonfiction. His sportswriting includes two volumes on basketball in the Pro Sports Halls of Fame series, as well as articles in *Sports Illustrated for Kids, National Geographic World,* and *Weekly Reader.* A graduate of the University of Connecticut, Burgan lives in Hartford.

Index